How to use this book

Follow the advice, in italics, given for you on each page.
Praise *the children at every step!*

Detailed guidance is provided in the Read Write Inc. Phonics Handbook.

7 reading activities

Children:

☆ *Practise reading the speed sounds.*

☆ *Read the green and red words for the Ditty.*

☆ *Listen as you read the introduction.*

☆ *Read the Ditty.*

☆ *Re-read the Ditty and discuss the 'questions to talk about'.*

☆ *Re-read the Ditty with fluency and expression.*

☆ *Practise reading the speed words.*

Speed Sounds

Consonants

Say the pure sounds (do not add 'uh').

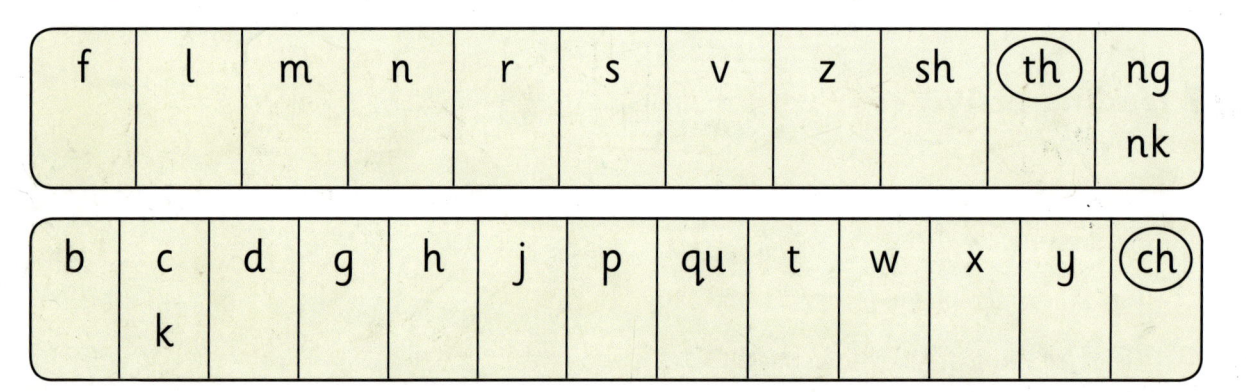

f	l	m	n	r	s	v	z	sh	(th)	ng
										nk

b	c	d	g	h	j	p	qu	t	w	x	y	(ch)
	k											

Vowels

Say the sounds in and out of order.

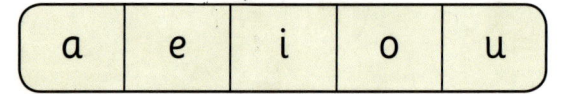

a	e	i	o	u

Each box contains only one sound. Focus sounds are circled.

Ditty 1 Pin it on

Green words

Read in Fred Talk (pure sounds).

tum pin yes not leg

on chin

Read the root word first and then with the ending.

that → that's

Ditty 1   Pin it on

Introduction
In this story, some children are playing a game called 'Pin the tail on the donkey'. They are blindfolded, and need to attach the tail to the right place. Let's see how they do!

pin it on

not on its leg

not on its chin

not on its tum

yes

that's it

pin it on

Ditty 2 Let's run

Green words

Read in Fred Talk (pure sounds).

zip run   up

Read the root word first and then with the ending.

let → let's

Red words

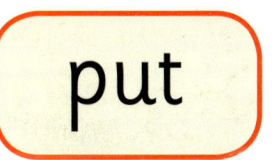

put

Ditty 2   Let's run

Introduction
Do you like snow? It can be exciting when it snows, but you need to be wearing the right clothes when you go out!

put it on

zip it up

put it on

put them on

let's run

Ditty 3 — A fun hat

Green words

Read in Fred Talk (pure sounds).

hen   red   hat   fox   sun

man   top   kid   fun   in

Ditty 3 A fun hat

Introduction
Do you have any hats? In this story, we see lots of special hats...

a hen in a red hat

a fox in a sun hat

a man in a top hat

a kid in a fun hat

Questions to talk about

Ditty 1
Where does the first girl pin the tail?
Do the children like playing the game?
What sort of games do you like to play at parties?

Ditty 2
What is the second thing that the boy puts on?
What do Mum and the boy do in the snow?
What do you put on when you go out in the snow?

Ditty 3
What type of hat does the fox have?
Which hat is your favourite?
How many other sorts of hats can you think of?

Speed words for Ditty 1

Children practise reading the words across the rows, down the columns and in and out of order clearly and quickly.

it	pin	its	on
yes	leg	chin	not

Speed words for Ditty 2

put	zip	on	up
them	it	run	let

Speed words for Ditty 3

in	fun	hen	a	top
red	hat	sun	fox	man